Percy Bysshe Shelley

Alastor

The Spirit of Solitude and Other Poems

Percy Bysshe Shelley

Alastor
The Spirit of Solitude and Other Poems

ISBN/EAN: 9783337006341

Printed in Europe, USA, Canada, Australia, Japan

Cover: Foto ©Thomas Meinert / pixelio.de

More available books at **www.hansebooks.com**

ALASTOR;

OR,

THE SPIRIT OF SOLITUDE:

AND OTHER POEMS.

BY

PERCY BYSSHE SHELLEY.

A FACSIMILE REPRINT OF THE ORIGINAL EDITION,
FIRST PUBLISHED IN 1816.

LONDON: 1885:
REEVES AND TURNER, 196, STRAND,
AND
B. DOBELL, 62, QUEEN'S CRESCENT, N.W.

This reprint of the original edition of Shelley's "Alastor" is restricted to 404 copies, viz.—
    4 copies on vellum.
    50 copies on Whatman's Hand-made Paper.
    350 copies on toned Paper.

PREFATORY NOTE.

THE excessive scarcity, and consequently the ever-increasing cost to the collector of the first editions of Shelley's writings, has suggested to me the idea of reprinting those editions exactly in their original form, and with all the peculiarities of their first appearance in print preserved as carefully as possible.

It must needs be interesting to every student of English literature to see in what form and apparel the works of our great authors made their first appearance in the world. The Shakspearean enthusiast, whose slender means forbid him to indulge the hope of ever obtaining a copy of the first folio edition of Shakespeare's works, is grateful to those who have provided him with a facsimile of it. So also with the lovers of Burns, Bunyan, Defoe, and other authors whose works have lately been reproduced in facsimile. This gratification of a laudable curiosity would alone be sufficient to justify the reproduction of works interesting from their merits, their age, or even their mere quaintness or rarity. But a better plea can be urged in favour of the practice. The real student will hardly ever be content with a text which has been "edited," however carefully the editor may have performed his task, when it is possible for him to get access to the original text. Of course I am not denying that many editors—and among them the editors of Shelley's works—have done most valuable services to their authors. But the ablest editors make occasional mistakes, and, however excellent and even indispensable their work may be, the student will still desire to have at hand the means of verifying their assertions, and of checking their conclusions. Facsimile reprints, provided they are executed with due care, furnish the means of doing this. They are justified therefore both on the grounds of sentiment and of practical use.

It is possible that some persons may doubt whether the time has yet arrived when it is desirable or necessary to reproduce the works of Shelley in facsimile. Perhaps I am mistaken in thinking that there is any general desire for such facsimiles; but I cannot doubt that Shelley's works are at least as worthy of reproduction as those of the authors whose writings have already achieved that distinction.

"Alastor" was already scarce in 1824, when Mrs. Shelley reprinted it in the "Posthumous Poems" expressly on account of its rarity. A copy of the original edition now fetches, on the rare occasions of its appearance in the auction room, from eight to ten pounds. This, of course, is a prohibitive price to all but wealthy collectors; and it seems reasonable to suppose, therefore, that those Shelleyites whose means are limited will not neglect the present opportunity of acquiring what is practically and substantially an original edition, at an almost nominal price.

PREFATORY NOTE.

I think I may say of the present reproduction that it is as near a facsimile of the original as it is possible to produce. The printing has been executed by Messrs. Whittingham and Co., whose reputation as careful and excellent typographers is too well established to need any eulogium from me: and I have revised the proof-sheets with the most anxious care. I suppose that no book has ever been published that was altogether free from mistakes, and therefore I dare not assert that this one will be altogether exempt from them: yet I shall certainly be surprised if any important errors are discovered in it.

It is no part of the present scheme to enter upon discussions regarding the difficulties of the text. These are fully debated in the editions of Messrs.

Rossetti and Forman. I may mention, however, that in the privately printed volume of Mr. Thomson's Writings on Shelley, there are some notes on " Alastor," which are well worth consulting.

In conclusion I beg to thank most heartily my friend, Thomas J. Wise, Esq., from whose excellent copy of "Alastor" the present edition has been reprinted.

BERTRAM DOBELL.

62, Queen's Crescent, Haverstock Hill.

ALASTOR;

OR,

THE SPIRIT OF SOLITUDE:

AND OTHER POEMS.

BY

PERCY BYSSHE SHELLEY.

LONDON:
PRINTED FOR BALDWIN, CRADOCK, AND JOY, PATER-
NOSTER ROW; AND CARPENTER AND SON,
OLD BOND-STREET:
By S. Hamilton, Weybridge, Surrey.

1816.

PREFACE.

The poem entitled 'Alastor,' may be considered as allegorical of one of the most interesting situations of the human mind. It represents a youth of uncorrupted feelings and adventurous genius led forth by an imagination inflamed and purified through familiarity with all that is excellent and majestic, to the contemplation of the universe. He drinks deep of the fountains of knowledge, and is still insatiate. The magnificence and beauty of the external world sinks profoundly into the frame of his conceptions, and affords to their modifications a variety not to be exhausted. So long as it is possible for his desires to point towards objects thus infinite and unmeasured, he is joyous, and tranquil, and self-possessed. But the period arrives when these objects cease to suffice. His mind is at length suddenly awakened and thirsts for intercourse with an intelligence similar to itself. He images to himself the Being whom he loves. Conversant with speculations of the sublimest and most perfect natures, the vision in which he embodies his own imaginations unites all of wonderful, or wise, or beautiful, which the poet, the philosopher, or the lover could depicture. The intellectual faculties, the imagination, the functions of sense, have their respective requisitions on the sympathy of corresponding powers in other human beings. The Poet is represented as uniting these requisitions, and attaching them to a single image. He seeks in vain for a prototype of his conception. Blasted by his disappointment, he descends to an untimely grave.

The picture is not barren of instruction to actual men. The Poet's self-centred seclusion was avenged by the furies of an irresistible passion pursuing him to speedy ruin. But that Power which strikes the luminaries of the world with sudden darkness and extinction, by awakening them to too exquisite a perception of its influences, dooms to a slow and poisonous decay those meaner spirits that dare to abjure its dominion. Their destiny is more abject and inglorious as their delinquency is more contemptible and pernicious. They who, deluded by no generous error, instigated by no sacred thirst of doubtful knowledge, duped by no illustrious superstition, loving nothing on this earth, and cherishing no hopes beyond, yet keep aloof from sympathies with their kind, rejoicing neither in human joy nor mourning with human grief; these, and such as they, have their apportioned curse. They languish, because none feel with them their common nature. They are morally dead. They are neither friends, nor lovers, nor fathers, nor citizens of the world, nor benefactors of their country. Among those who attempt to exist without human sympathy, the pure and tender-hearted perish through the intensity and passion of their search after its communities, when the vacancy of their spirit suddenly makes itself felt. All else, selfish, blind, and torpid, are those unforeseeing multitudes who constitute, together with their own, the lasting misery and loneliness of the world. Those who love not their fellow-beings, live unfruitful lives, and prepare for their old age a miserable grave.

> 'The good die first,
> And those whose hearts are dry as summer dust,
> Burn to the socket!'

The Fragment, entitled 'THE DÆMON OF THE WORLD,' is a detached part of a poem which the author does not intend for publication. The metre in which it is composed is that of Samson Agonistes and the Italian pastoral drama, and may be considered as the natural measure into which poetical conceptions, expressed in harmonious language, necessarily fall.

December 14, 1815.

ALASTOR;

OR,

THE SPIRIT OF SOLITUDE.

Nondum amabam, et amare amabam, quærebam quid amarem, amans mare.

Confess. St. August.

ALASTOR;

OR,

THE SPIRIT OF SOLITUDE.

EARTH, ocean, air, beloved brotherhood!
If our great Mother has imbued my soul
With aught of natural piety to feel
Your love, and recompense the boon with mine;
If dewy morn, and odorous noon, and even,
With sunset and its gorgeous ministers,
And solemn midnight's tingling silentness;

If autumn's hollow sighs in the sere wood,
And winter robing with pure snow and crowns
Of starry ice the gray grass and bare boughs;
If spring's voluptuous pantings when she breathes
Her first sweet kisses, have been dear to me;
If no bright bird, insect, or gentle beast
I consciously have injured, but still loved
And cherished these my kindred; then forgive
This boast, beloved brethren, and withdraw
No portion of your wonted favour now!

Mother of this unfathomable world!
Favour my solemn song, for I have loved
Thee ever, and thee only; I have watched
Thy shadow, and the darkness of thy steps,
And my heart ever gazes on the depth

Of thy deep mysteries. I have made my bed
In charnels and on coffins, where black death
Keeps record of the trophies won from thee,
Hoping to still these obstinate questionings
Of thee and thine, by forcing some lone ghost
Thy messenger, to render up the tale
Of what we are. In lone and silent hours,
When night makes a weird sound of its own stillness,
Like an inspired and desperate alchymist
Staking his very life on some dark hope,
Have I mixed awful talk and asking looks
With my most innocent love, until strange tears
Uniting with those breathless kisses, made
Such magic as compels the charmed night
To render up thy charge : . . . and, though ne'er yet

Thou hast unveil'd thy inmost sanctuary;
Enough from incommunicable dream,
And twilight phantasms, and deep noonday thought,
Has shone within me, that serenely now
And moveless, as a long-forgotten lyre
Suspended in the solitary dome
Of some mysterious and deserted fane,
I wait thy breath, Great Parent, that my strain
May modulate with murmurs of the air,
And motions of the forests and the sea,
And voice of living beings, and woven hymns
Of night and day, and the deep heart of man.

   There was a Poet whose untimely tomb
No human hands with pious reverence reared,
But the charmed eddies of autumnal winds

Built o'er his mouldering bones a pyramid
Of mouldering leaves in the waste wilderness :—
A lovely youth,—no mourning maiden decked
With weeping flowers, or votive cypress wreath,
The lone couch of his everlasting sleep :—
Gentle, and brave, and generous,—no lorn bard
Breathed o'er his dark fate one melodious sigh :
He lived, he died, he sung, in solitude.
Strangers have wept to hear his passionate notes,
And virgins, as unknown he past, have pined
And wasted for fond love of his wild eyes.
The fire of those soft orbs has ceased to burn,
And Silence, too enamoured of that voice,
Locks its mute music in her rugged cell.

 By solemn vision, and bright silver dream,

His infancy was nurtured. Every sight
And sound from the vast earth and ambient air,
Sent to his heart its choicest impulses.
The fountains of divine philosophy
Fled not his thirsting lips, and all of great,
Or good, or lovely, which the sacred past
In truth or fable consecrates, he felt
And knew. When early youth had past, he left
His cold fireside and alienated home
To seek strange truths in undiscovered lands.
Many a wide waste and tangled wilderness
Has lured his fearless steps; and he has bought
With his sweet voice and eyes, from savage men,
His rest and food. Nature's most secret steps
He like her shadow has pursued, where'er

The red volcano overcanopies

Its fields of snow and pinnacles of ice

With burning smoke, or where bitumen lakes

On black bare pointed islets ever beat

With sluggish surge, or where the secret caves

Rugged and dark, winding among the springs

Of fire and poison, inaccessible

To avarice or pride, their starry domes

Of diamond and of gold expand above

Numberless and immeasurable halls,

Frequent with crystal column, and clear shrines

Of pearl, and thrones radiant with chrysolite.

Nor had that scene of ampler majesty

Than gems or gold, the varying roof of heaven

And the green earth lost in his heart its claims

To love and wonder; he would linger long
In lonesome vales, making the wild his home,
Until the doves and squirrels would partake
From his innocuous hand his bloodless food,
Lured by the gentle meaning of his looks,
And the wild antelope, that starts whene'er
The dry leaf rustles in the brake, suspend
Her timid steps to gaze upon a form
More graceful than her own.

       His wandering step
Obedient to high thoughts, has visited
The awful ruins of the days of old:
Athens, and Tyre, and Balbec, and the waste
Where stood Jerusalem, the fallen towers
Of Babylon, the eternal pyramids,

Memphis and Thebes, and whatsoe'er of strange
Sculptured on alabaster obelisk,
Or jasper tomb, or mutilated sphynx,
Dark Æthiopia in her desert hills
Conceals. Among the ruined temples there,
Stupendous columns, and wild images
Of more than man, where marble dæmons watch
The Zodiac's brazen mystery, and dead men
Hang their mute thoughts on the mute walls around,
He lingered, poring on memorials
Of the world's youth, through the long burning day
Gazed on those speechless shapes, nor, when the moon
Filled the mysterious halls with floating shades
Suspended he that task, but ever gazed
And gazed, till meaning on his vacant mind

Flashed like strong inspiration, and he saw
The thrilling secrets of the birth of time.

  Meanwhile an Arab maiden brought his food,
Her daily portion, from her father's tent,
And spread her matting for his couch, and stole
From duties and repose to tend his steps :—
Enamoured, yet not daring for deep awe
To speak her love :—and watched his nightly sleep,
Sleepless herself, to gaze upon his lips
Parted in slumber, whence the regular breath
Of innocent dreams arose : then, when red morn
Made paler the pale moon, to her cold home
Wildered, and wan, and panting, she returned.

  The Poet wandering on, through Arabie
And Persia, and the wild Carmanian waste,

And o'er the aërial mountains which pour down
Indus and Oxus from their icy caves,
In joy and exultation held his way;
Till in the vale of Cashmire, far within
Its loneliest dell, where odorous plants entwine
Beneath the hollow rocks a natural bower,
Beside a sparkling rivulet he stretched
His languid limbs. A vision on his sleep
There came, a dream of hopes that never yet
Had flushed his cheek. He dreamed a veiled maid
Sate near him, talking in low solemn tones.
Her voice was like the voice of his own soul
Heard in the calm of thought; its music long,
Like woven sounds of streams and breezes, held
His inmost sense suspended in its web

Of many-coloured woof and shifting hues.

Knowledge and truth and virtue were her theme,

And lofty hopes of divine liberty,

Thoughts the most dear to him, and poesy,

Herself a poet. Soon the solemn mood

Of her pure mind kindled through all her frame

A permeating fire : wild numbers then

She raised, with voice stifled in tremulous sobs

Subdued by its own pathos : her fair hands

Were bare alone, sweeping from some strange harp

Strange symphony, and in their branching veins

The eloquent blood told an ineffable tale.

The beating of her heart was heard to fill

The pauses of her music, and her breath

Tumultuously accorded with those fits

Of intermitted song. Sudden she rose,
As if her heart impatiently endured
Its bursting burthen : at the sound he turned,
And saw by the warm light of their own life
Her glowing limbs beneath the sinuous veil
Of woven wind, her outspread arms now bare,
Her dark locks floating in the breath of night,
Her beamy bending eyes, her parted lips
Outstretched, and pale, and quivering eagerly.
His strong heart sunk and sickened with excess
Of love. He reared his shuddering limbs and quelled
His gasping breath, and spread his arms to meet
Her panting bosom : . . . she drew back a while,
Then, yielding to the irresistible joy,
With frantic gesture and short breathless cry

Folded his frame in her dissolving arms.

Now blackness veiled his dizzy eyes, and night
Involved and swallowed up the vision; sleep,
Like a dark flood suspended in its course,
Rolled back its impulse on his vacant brain.

Roused by the shock he started from his trance—
The cold white light of morning, the blue moon
Low in the west, the clear and garish hills,
The distinct valley and the vacant woods,
Spread round him where he stood. Whither have fled
The hues of heaven that canopied his bower
Of yesternight? The sounds that soothed his sleep,
The mystery and the majesty of Earth,
The joy, the exultation? His wan eyes
Gaze on the empty scene as vacantly

As ocean's moon looks on the moon in heaven.

The spirit of sweet human love has sent

A vision to the sleep of him who spurned

Her choicest gifts.   He eagerly pursues

Beyond the realms of dream that fleeting shade ;

He overleaps the bounds.   Alas ! alas !

Were limbs, and breath, and being intertwined

Thus treacherously ?   Lost, lost, for ever lost,

In the wide pathless desert of dim sleep,

That beautiful shape !   Does the dark gate of death

Conduct to thy mysterious paradise,

O Sleep ?   Does the bright arch of rainbow clouds,

And pendent mountains seen in the calm lake,

Lead only to a black and watery depth,

While death's blue vault, with loathliest vapours hung,

Where every shade which the foul grave exhales
Hides its dead eye from the detested day,
Conduct, O Sleep, to thy delightful realms?
This doubt with sudden tide flowed on his heart,
The insatiate hope which it awakened, stung
His brain even like despair.

     While day-light held
The sky, the Poet kept mute conference
With his still soul. At night the passion came,
Like the fierce fiend of a distempered dream,
And shook him from his rest, and led him forth
Into the darkness.—As an eagle grasped
In folds of the green serpent, feels her breast
Burn with the poison, and precipitates
Through night and day, tempest, and calm, and cloud,

Frantic with dizzying anguish, her blind flight
O'er the wide aëry wilderness: thus driven
By the bright shadow of that lovely dream,
Beneath the cold glare of the desolate night,
Through tangled swamps and deep precipitous dells,
Startling with careless step the moon-light snake,
He fled. Red morning dawned upon his flight,
Shedding the mockery of its vital hues
Upon his cheek of death. He wandered on
Till vast Aornos seen from Petra's steep
Hung o'er the low horizon like a cloud;
Through Balk, and where the desolated tombs
Of Parthian kings scatter to every wind
Their wasting dust, wildly he wandered on,
Day after day, a weary waste of hours,

Bearing within his life the brooding care

That ever fed on its decaying flame.

And now his limbs were lean; his scattered hair

Sered by the autumn of strange suffering

Sung dirges in the wind; his listless hand

Hung like dead bone within its withered skin;

Life, and the lustre that consumed it, shone

As in a furnace burning secretly

From his dark eyes alone. The cottagers,

Who ministered with human charity

His human wants, beheld with wondering awe

Their fleeting visitant. The mountaineer,

Encountering on some dizzy precipice

That spectral form, deemed that the Spirit of wind

With lightning eyes, and eager breath, and feet

Disturbing not the drifted snow, had paused
In its career: the infant would conceal
His troubled visage in his mother's robe
In terror at the glare of those wild eyes,
To remember their strange light in many a dream
Of after-times; but youthful maidens, taught
By nature, would interpret half the woe
That wasted him, would call him with false names
Brother, and friend, would press his pallid hand
At parting, and watch, dim through tears, the path
Of his departure from their father's door.

 At length upon the lone Chorasmian shore
He paused, a wide and melancholy waste
Of putrid marshes. A strong impulse urged
His steps to the sea-shore. A swan was there,

Beside a sluggish stream among the reeds.

It rose as he approached, and with strong wings

Scaling the upward sky, bent its bright course

High over the immeasurable main.

His eyes pursued its flight.—" Thou hast a home,

Beautiful bird; thou voyagest to thine home,

Where thy sweet mate will twine her downy neck

With thine, and welcome thy return with eyes

Bright in the lustre of their own fond joy.

And what am I that I should linger here,

With voice far sweeter than thy dying notes,

Spirit more vast than thine, frame more attuned

To beauty, wasting these surpassing powers

In the deaf air, to the blind earth, and heaven

That echoes not my thoughts?" A gloomy smile

Of desperate hope wrinkled his quivering lips.

For sleep, he knew, kept most relentlessly

Its precious charge, and silent death exposed,

Faithless perhaps as sleep, a shadowy lure,

With doubtful smile mocking its own strange charms.

    Startled by his own thoughts he looked around.

There was no fair fiend near him, not a sight

Or sound of awe but in his own deep mind.

A little shallop floating near the shore

Caught the impatient wandering of his gaze.

It had been long abandoned, for its sides

Gaped wide with many a rift, and its frail joints

Swayed with the undulations of the tide.

A restless impulse urged him to embark

And meet lone Death on the drear ocean's waste;

For well he knew that mighty Shadow loves
The slimy caverns of the populous deep.

 The day was fair and sunny, sea and sky
Drank its inspiring radiance, and the wind
Swept strongly from the shore, blackening the waves.
Following his eager soul, the wanderer,
Leaped in the boat, he spread his cloak aloft
On the bare mast, and took his lonely seat,
And felt the boat speed o'er the tranquil sea
Like a torn cloud before the hurricane.

 As one that in a silver vision floats
Obedient to the sweep of odorous winds
Upon resplendent clouds, so rapidly
Along the dark and ruffled waters fled
The straining boat.—A whirlwind swept it on,

With fierce gusts and precipitating force,
Through the white ridges of the chafed sea.
The waves arose. Higher and higher still
Their fierce necks writhed beneath the tempest's scourge
Like serpents struggling in a vulture's grasp.
Calm and rejoicing in the fearful war
Of wave ruining on wave, and blast on blast
Descending, and black flood on whirlpool driven
With dark obliterating course, he sate:
As if their genii were the ministers
Appointed to conduct him to the light
Of those beloved eyes, the Poet sate
Holding the steady helm. Evening came on,
The beams of sunset hung their rainbow hues
High 'mid the shifting domes of sheeted spray

That canopied his path o'er the waste deep;
Twilight, ascending slowly from the east,
Entwin'd in duskier wreaths her braided locks
O'er the fair front and radiant eyes of day;
Night followed, clad with stars. On every side
More horribly the multitudinous streams
Of ocean's mountainous waste to mutual war
Rushed in dark tumult thundering, as to mock
The calm and spangled sky. The little boat
Still fled before the storm; still fled, like foam
Down the steep cataract of a wintry river;
Now pausing on the edge of the riven wave;
Now leaving far behind the bursting mass
That fell, convulsing ocean. Safely fled—
As if that frail and wasted human form,

Had been an elemental god.

     At midnight
The moon arose: and lo! the etherial cliffs
Of Caucasus, whose icy summits shone
Among the stars like sunlight, and around
Whose cavern'd base the whirlpools and the waves
Bursting and eddying irresistibly
Rage and resound for ever.—Who shall save?—
The boat fled on,—the boiling torrent drove,—
The crags closed round with black and jagged arms,
The shattered mountain overhung the sea,
And faster still, beyond all human speed,
Suspended on the sweep of the smooth wave,
The little boat was driven. A cavern there
Yawned, and amid its slant and winding depths

Ingulphed the rushing sea. The boat fled on
With unrelaxing speed.—' Vision and Love!'
The Poet cried aloud, 'I have beheld
The path of thy departure. Sleep and death
Shall not divide us long!'

       The boat pursued
The windings of the cavern. Day-light shone
At length upon that gloomy river's flow;
Now, where the fiercest war among the waves
Is calm, on the unfathomable stream
The boat moved slowly. Where the mountain, riven,
Exposed those black depths to the azure sky,
Ere yet the flood's enormous volume fell
Even to the base of Caucasus, with sound
That shook the everlasting rocks, the mass

Filled with one whirlpool all that ample chasm;
Stair above stair the eddying waters rose,
Circling immeasurably fast, and laved
With alternating dash the knarled roots
Of mighty trees, that stretched their giant arms
In darkness over it. I' the midst was left,
Reflecting, yet distorting every cloud,
A pool of treacherous and tremendous calm.
Seized by the sway of the ascending stream,
With dizzy swiftness, round, and round, and round,
Ridge after ridge the straining boat arose,
Till on the verge of the extremest curve,
Where, through an opening of the rocky bank,
The waters overflow, and a smooth spot
Of glassy quiet mid those battling tides

Is left, the boat paused shuddering.—Shall it sink

Down the abyss? Shall the reverting stress

Of that resistless gulph embosom it?

Now shall it fall?—A wandering stream of wind,

Breathed from the west, has caught the expanded sail,

And, lo! with gentle motion, between banks

Of mossy slope, and on a placid stream,

Beneath a woven grove it sails, and, hark!

The ghastly torrent mingles its far roar

With the breeze murmuring in the musical woods.

Where the embowering trees recede, and leave

A little space of green expanse, the cove

Is closed by meeting banks, whose yellow flowers

For ever gaze on their own drooping eyes,

Reflected in the crystal calm. The wave

Of the boat's motion marred their pensive task,

Which nought but vagrant bird, or wanton wind,

Or falling spear-grass, or their own decay

Had e'er disturbed before. The Poet longed

To deck with their bright hues his withered hair,

But on his heart its solitude returned,

And he forbore. Not the strong impulse hid

In those flushed cheeks, bent eyes, and shadowy frame,

Had yet performed its ministry: it hung

Upon his life, as lightning in a cloud

Gleams, hovering ere it vanish, ere the floods

Of night close over it.

     The noonday sun

Now shone upon the forest, one vast mass

Of mingling shade, whose brown magnificence

A narrow vale embosoms. There, huge caves,
Scooped in the dark base of their aëry rocks
Mocking its moans, respond and roar for ever.
The meeting boughs and implicated leaves
Wove twilight o'er the Poet's path, as led
By love, or dream, or god, or mightier Death,
He sought in Nature's dearest haunt, some bank,
Her cradle, and his sepulchre. More dark
And dark the shades accumulate. The oak,
Expanding its immense and knotty arms,
Embraces the light beech. The pyramids
Of the tall cedar overarching, frame
Most solemn domes within, and far below,
Like clouds suspended in an emerald sky,
The ash and the acacia floating hang

Tremulous and pale. Like restless serpents, clothed
In rainbow and in fire, the parasites,
Starred with ten thousand blossoms, flow around
The gray trunks, and, as gamesome infants' eyes,
With gentle meanings, and most innocent wiles,
Fold their beams round the hearts of those that love,
These twine their tendrils with the wedded boughs
Uniting their close union; the woven leaves
Make net-work of the dark blue light of day,
And the night's noontide clearness, mutable
As shapes in the weird clouds. Soft mossy lawns
Beneath these canopies extend their swells,
Fragrant with perfumed herbs, and eyed with blooms
Minute yet beautiful. One darkest glen
Sends from its woods of musk-rose, twined with jasmine,

A soul-dissolving odour, to invite
To some more lovely mystery. Through the dell,
Silence and Twilight here, twin-sisters, keep
Their noonday watch, and sail among the shades,
Like vaporous shapes half seen; beyond, a well,
Dark, gleaming, and of most translucent wave,
Images all the woven boughs above,
And each depending leaf, and every speck
Of azure sky, darting between their chasms;
Nor aught else in the liquid mirror laves
Its portraiture, but some inconstant star
Between one foliaged lattice twinkling fair,
Or, painted bird, sleeping beneath the moon,
Or gorgeous insect floating motionless,
Unconscious of the day, ere yet his wings

Have spread their glories to the gaze of noon.

Hither the Poet came. His eyes beheld
Their own wan light through the reflected lines
Of his thin hair, distinct in the dark depth
Of that still fountain; as the human heart,
Gazing in dreams over the gloomy grave,
Sees its own treacherous likeness there. He heard
The motion of the leaves, the grass that sprung
Startled and glanced and trembled even to feel
An unaccustomed presence, and the sound
Of the sweet brook that from the secret springs
Of that dark fountain rose. A Spirit seemed
To stand beside him—clothed in no bright robes
Of shadowy silver or enshrining light,
Borrowed from aught the visible world affords

Of grace, or majesty, or mystery ;—
But, undulating woods, and silent well,
And leaping rivulet, and evening gloom
Now deepening the dark shades, for speech assuming
Held commune with him, as if he and it
Were all that was,—only . . . when his regard
Was raised by intense pensiveness, . . . two eyes,
Two starry eyes, hung in the gloom of thought,
And seemed with their serene and azure smiles
To beckon him.

     Obedient to the light
That shone with his soul, he went, pursuing
The windings of the dell.—The rivulet
Wanton and wild, through many a green ravine
Beneath the forest flowed. Sometimes it fell

Among the moss with hollow harmony
Dark and profound.   Now on the polished stones
It danced ; like childhood laughing as it went :
Then, through the plain in tranquil wanderings crept,
Reflecting every herb and drooping bud
That overhung its quietness.—' O stream !
Whose source is inaccessibly profound,
Whither do thy mysterious waters tend?
Thou imagest my life.   Thy darksome stillness,
Thy dazzling waves, thy loud and hollow gulphs,
Thy searchless fountain, and invisible course
Have each their type in me : and the wide sky,
And measureless ocean may declare as soon
What oozy cavern or what wandering cloud
Contains thy waters, as the universe

Tell where these living thoughts reside, when stretched
Upon thy flowers my bloodless limbs shall waste
I' the passing wind!'

      Beside the grassy shore
Of the small stream he went; he did impress
On the green moss his tremulous step, that caught
Strong shuddering from his burning limbs. As one
Roused by some joyous madness from the couch
Of fever, he did move; yet, not like him,
Forgetful of the grave, where, when the flame
Of his frail exultation shall be spent,
He must descend. With rapid steps he went
Beneath the shade of trees, beside the flow
Of the wild babbling rivulet, and now
The forest's solemn canopies were changed

For the uniform and lightsome evening sky.
Gray rocks did peep from the spare moss, and stemmed
The struggling brook : tall spires of windlestrae
Threw their thin shadows down the rugged slope,
And nought but knarled roots of ancient pines
Branchless and blasted, clenched with grasping roots
The unwilling soil. A gradual change was here,
Yet ghastly. For, as fast years flow away,
The smooth brow gathers, and the hair grows thin
And white, and where irradiate dewy eyes
Had shone, gleam stony orbs :—so from his steps
Bright flowers departed, and the beautiful shade
Of the green groves, with all their odorous winds
And musical motions. Calm, he still pursued
The stream, that with a larger volume now

Rolled through the labyrinthine dell; and there
Fretted a path through its descending curves
With its wintry speed. On every side now rose
Rocks, which, in unimaginable forms,
Lifted their black and barren pinnacles
In the light of evening, and its precipice
Obscuring the ravine, disclosed above,
Mid toppling stones, black gulphs and yawning caves,
Whose windings gave ten thousand various tongues
To the loud stream. Lo! where the pass expands
Its stony jaws, the abrupt mountain breaks,
And seems, with its accumulated crags,
To overhang the world: for wide expand
Beneath the wan stars and descending moon
Islanded seas, blue mountains, mighty streams,

Dim tracts and vast, robed in the lustrous gloom
Of leaden-coloured even, and fiery hills
Mingling their flames with twilight, on the verge
Of the remote horizon.   The near scene,
In naked and severe simplicity,
Made contrast with the universe.   A pine,
Rock-rooted, stretched athwart the vacancy
Its swinging boughs, to each inconstant blast
Yielding one only response, at each pause
In most familiar cadence, with the howl
The thunder and the hiss of homeless streams
Mingling its solemn song, whilst the broad river,
Foaming and hurrying o'er its rugged path,
Fell into that immeasurable void
Scattering its waters to the passing winds.

Yet the gray precipice and solemn pine
And torrent, were not all;—one silent nook
Was there. Even on the edge of that vast mountain,
Upheld by knotty roots and fallen rocks,
It overlooked in its serenity
The dark earth, and the bending vault of stars.
It was a tranquil spot, that seemed to smile
Even in the lap of horror. Ivy clasped
The fissured stones with its entwining arms,
And did embower with leaves for ever green,
And berries dark, the smooth and even space
Of its inviolated floor, and here
The children of the autumnal whirlwind bore,
In wanton sport, those bright leaves, whose decay,
Red, yellow, or etherially pale,

Rivals the pride of summer. 'Tis the haunt
Of every gentle wind, whose breath can teach
The wilds to love tranquillity. One step,
One human step alone, has ever broken
The stillness of its solitude :—one voice
Alone inspired its echoes,—even that voice
Which hither came, floating among the winds,
And led the loveliest among human forms
To make their wild haunts the depository
Of all the grace and beauty that endued
Its motions, render up its majesty,
Scatter its music on the unfeeling storm,
And to the damp leaves and blue cavern mould,
Nurses of rainbow flowers and branching moss,
Commit the colours of that varying cheek,

That snowy breast, those dark and drooping eyes.

The dim and horned moon hung low, and poured
A sea of lustre on the horizon's verge
That overflowed its mountains. Yellow mist
Filled the unbounded atmosphere, and drank
Wan moonlight even to fullness: not a star
Shone, not a sound was heard; the very winds,
Danger's grim playmates, on that precipice
Slept, clasped in his embrace.—O, storm of death!
Whose sightless speed divides this sullen night:
And thou, colossal Skeleton, that, still
Guiding its irresistible career
In thy devastating omnipotence,
Art king of this frail world, from the red field
Of slaughter, from the reeking hospital,

The patriot's sacred couch, the snowy bed
Of innocence, the scaffold and the throne,
A mighty voice invokes thee. Ruin calls
His brother Death. A rare and regal prey
He hath prepared, prowling around the world;
Glutted with which thou mayst repose, and men
Go to their graves like flowers or creeping worms,
Nor ever more offer at thy dark shrine
The unheeded tribute of a broken heart.

When on the threshold of the green recess
The wanderer's footsteps fell, he knew that death
Was on him. Yet a little, ere it fled,
Did he resign his high and holy soul
To images of the majestic past,
That paused within his passive being now,

Like winds that bear sweet music, when they breathe
Through some dim latticed chamber. He did place
His pale lean hand upon the rugged trunk
Of the old pine. Upon an ivied stone
Reclined his languid head, his limbs did rest,
Diffused and motionless, on the smooth brink
Of that obscurest chasm;—and thus he lay,
Surrendering to their final impulses
The hovering powers of life. Hope and despair,
The torturers, slept; no mortal pain or fear
Marred his repose, the influxes of sense,
And his own being unalloyed by pain,
Yet feebler and more feeble, calmly fed
The stream of thought, till he lay breathing there
At peace, and faintly smiling:—his last sight

Was the great moon, which o'er the western line
Of the wide world her mighty horn suspended,
With whose dun beams inwoven darkness seemed
To mingle. Now upon the jagged hills
It rests, and still as the divided frame
Of the vast meteor sunk, the Poet's blood,
That ever beat in mystic sympathy
With nature's ebb and flow, grew feebler still:
And when two lessening points of light alone
Gleamed through the darkness, the alternate gasp
Of his faint respiration scarce did stir
The stagnate night:—till the minutest ray
Was quenched, the pulse yet lingered in his heart.
It paused—it fluttered. But when heaven remained
Utterly black, the murky shades involved

An image, silent, cold, and motionless,
As their own voiceless earth and vacant air.
Even as a vapour fed with golden beams
That ministered on sunlight, ere the west
Eclipses it, was now that wonderous frame—
No sense, no motion, no divinity—
A fragile lute, on whose harmonious strings
The breath of heaven did wander—a bright stream
Once fed with many-voiced waves—a dream
Of youth, which night and time have quenched forever,
Still, dark, and dry, and unremembered now.

 O, for Medea's wondrous alchemy,
Which wheresoe'er it fell made the earth gleam
With bright flowers, and the wintry boughs exhale
From vernal blooms fresh fragrance! O, that God,

Profuse of poisons, would concede the chalice
Which but one living man has drained, who now,
Vessel of deathless wrath, a slave that feels
No proud exemption in the blighting curse
He bears, over the world wanders for ever,
Lone as incarnate death! O, that the dream
Of dark magician in his visioned cave,
Raking the cinders of a crucible
For life and power, even when his feeble hand
Shakes in its last decay, were the true law
Of this so lovely world! But thou art fled
Like some frail exhalation; which the dawn
Robes in its golden beams,—ah! thou hast fled!
The brave, the gentle, and the beautiful,
The child of grace and genius. Heartless things

Are done and said i' the world, and many worms
And beasts and men live on, and mighty Earth
From sea and mountain, city and wilderness,
In vesper low or joyous orison,
Lifts still its solemn voice :—but thou art fled—
Thou canst no longer know or love the shapes
Of this phantasmal scene, who have to thee
Been purest ministers, who are, alas!
Now thou art not. Upon those pallid lips
So sweet even in their silence, on those eyes
That image sleep in death, upon that form
Yet safe from the worm's outrage, let no tear
Be shed—not even in thought. Nor, when those hues
Are gone, and those divinest lineaments,
Worn by the senseless wind, shall live alone

In the frail pauses of this simple strain,

Let not high verse, mourning the memory

Of that which is no more, or painting's woe

Or sculpture, speak in feeble imagery

Their own cold powers. Art and eloquence,

And all the shews o' the world are frail and vain

To weep a loss that turns their lights to shade.

It is a woe too 'deep for tears,' when all

Is reft at once, when some surpassing Spirit,

Whose light adorned the world around it, leaves

Those who remain behind, not sobs or groans,

The passionate tumult of a clinging hope ;

But pale despair and cold tranquillity,

Nature's vast frame, the web of human things,

Birth and the grave, that are not as they were.

POEMS.

POEMS.

ΔΑΚΡΥΕΙ ΛΙΟΙΣΩ ΠΟΤΜΟΝ ΑΠΟΤΜΟΝ.

O! there are spirits of the air,

 And genii of the evening breeze,

 And gentle ghosts, with eyes as fair

  As star-beams among twilight trees :—

Such lovely ministers to meet

Oft hast thou turned from men thy lonely feet.

 With mountain winds, and babbling springs,

  And moonlight seas, that are the voice

 Of these inexplicable things

  Thou didst hold commune, and rejoice

When they did answer thee; but they
Cast, like a worthless boon, thy love away.'

And thou hast sought in starry eyes
    Beams that were never meant for thine
Another's wealth :—tame sacrifice
    To a fond faith! still dost thou pine?
Still dost thou hope that greeting hands,
Voice, looks, or lips, may answer thy demands?

Ah! wherefore didst thou build thine hope
    On the false earth's inconstancy?
Did thine own mind afford no scope
    Of love, or moving thoughts to thee?
That natural scenes or human smiles
Could steal the power to wind thee in their wiles.

Yes, all the faithless smiles are fled
   Whose falsehood left thee broken-hearted;
The glory of the moon is dead;
   Night's ghosts and dreams have now departed;
Thine own soul still is true to thee,
But changed to a foul fiend through misery.

This fiend, whose ghastly presence ever
   Beside thee like thy shadow hangs,
Dream not to chase;—the mad endeavour
   Would scourge thee to severer pangs.
Be as thou art. Thy settled fate,
Dark as it is, all change would aggravate.

STANZAS.—APRIL, 1814.

Away! the moor is dark beneath the moon,
    Rapid clouds have drank the last pale beam of even:
Away! the gathering winds will call the darkness soon,
    And profoundest midnight shroud the serene lights of heaven.

Pause not! The time is past! Every voice cries, Away!
    Tempt not with one last tear thy friend's ungentle mood:
Thy lover's eye, so glazed and cold, dares not entreat thy stay:
    Duty and dereliction guide thee back to solitude.

Away, away! to thy sad and silent home;
Pour bitter tears on its desolated hearth;
Watch the dim shades as like ghosts they go and come,
And complicate strange webs of melancholy mirth.
The leaves of wasted autumn woods shall float around
thine head:
The blooms of dewy spring shall gleam beneath thy
feet:
But thy soul or this world must fade in the frost that
binds the dead,
Ere midnight's frown and morning's smile, ere thou
and peace may meet.

The cloud shadows of midnight possess their own
repose,

For the weary winds are silent, or the moon is in
    the deep:
Some respite to its turbulence unresting ocean knows;
    Whatever moves, or toils, or grieves, hath its ap-
    pointed sleep.
Thou in the grave shalt rest—yet till the phantoms flee
    Which that house and heath and garden made dear
    to thee erewhile,
Thy remembrance, and repentance, and deep musings
    are not free
From the music of two voices and the light of one
    sweet smile.

MUTABILITY.

We are as clouds that veil the midnight moon;
  How restlessly they speed, and gleam, and quiver,
Streaking the darkness radiantly!—yet soon
  Night closes round, and they are lost for ever:

Or like forgotten lyres, whose dissonant strings
  Give various response to each varying blast,
To whose frail frame no second motion brings
  One mood or modulation like the last.

We rest.—A dream has power to poison sleep;
  We rise.—One wandering thought pollutes the day;

We feel, conceive or reason, laugh or weep;

Embrace fond woe, or cast our cares away:

It is the same!—For, be it joy or sorrow,

The path of its departure still is free:

Man's yesterday may ne'er be like his morrow;

Nought may endure but Mutability.

THERE IS NO WORK, NOR DEVICE, NOR KNOWLEDGE, NOR WISDOM, IN THE GRAVE, WHITHER THOU GOEST.
Ecclesiastes.

The pale, the cold, and the moony smile
    Which the meteor beam of a starless night
Sheds on a lonely and sea-girt isle,
    Ere the dawning of morn's undoubted light,
Is the flame of life so fickle and wan
That flits round our steps till their strength is gone.

O man! hold thee on in courage of soul
    Through the stormy shades of thy worldly way,
And the billows of cloud that around thee roll
    Shall sleep in the light of a wondrous day,
Where hell and heaven shall leave thee free
To the universe of destiny.

This world is the nurse of all we know,

    This world is the mother of all we feel,

And the coming of death is a fearful blow

    To a brain unencompassed with nerves of steel;

When all that we know, or feel, or see,

Shall pass like an unreal mystery.

The secret things of the grave are there,

    Where all but this frame must surely be,

Though the fine-wrought eye and the wondrous ear

    No longer will live to hear or to see

All that is great and all that is strange

In the boundless realm of unending change.

Who telleth a tale of unspeaking death?

    Who lifteth the veil of what is to come?

Who painteth the shadows that are beneath

   The wide-winding cave of the peopled tomb?

Or uniteth the hopes of what shall be

With the fears and the love for that which we see?

A SUMMER-EVENING CHURCH-YARD,

LECHLADE, GLOUCESTERSHIRE.

The wind has swept from the wide atmosphere
Each vapour that obscured the sunset's ray;
And pallid evening twines its beaming hair
In duskier braids around the languid eyes of day:
Silence and twilight, unbeloved of men,
Creep hand in hand from yon obscurest glen.

They breathe their spells towards the departing day,
Encompassing the earth, air, stars, and sea;

Light, sound, and motion own the potent sway,

Responding to the charm with its own mystery.

The winds are still, or the dry church-tower grass

Knows not their gentle motions as they pass.

Thou too, aerial Pile! whose pinnacles

Point from one shrine like pyramids of fire,

Obeyest in silence their sweet solemn spells,

Clothing in hues of heaven thy dim and distant spire,

Around whose lessening and invisible height

Gather among the stars the clouds of night.

The dead are sleeping in their sepulchres:

And, mouldering as they sleep, a thrilling sound

Half sense, half thought, among the darkness stirs,

Breathed from their wormy beds all living things around,

And mingling with the still night and mute sky

Its awful hush is felt inaudibly.

Thus solemnized and softened, death is mild

And terrorless as this serenest night:

Here could I hope, like some enquiring child

Sporting on graves, that death did hide from human sight

Sweet secrets, or beside its breathless sleep

That loveliest dreams perpetual watch did keep.

TO WORDSWORTH.

Poet of Nature, thou hast wept to know

That things depart which never may return:

Childhood and youth, friendship and love's first glow,

Have fled like sweet dreams, leaving thee to mourn.

These common woes I feel. One loss is mine

Which thou too feel'st, yet I alone deplore.

Thou wert as a lone star, whose light did shine

On some frail bark in winter's midnight roar:

Thou hast like to a rock-built refuge stood

Above the blind and battling multitude:

In honoured poverty thy voice did weave

Songs consecrate to truth and liberty,—

Deserting these, thou leavest me to grieve,

Thus having been, that thou shouldst cease to be.

FEELINGS OF A REPUBLICAN

ON THE FALL OF BONAPARTE.

I HATED thee, fallen tyrant! I did groan
To think that a most unambitious slave,
Like thou, shouldst dance and revel on the grave
Of Liberty. Thou mightst have built thy throne
Where it had stood even now: thou didst prefer
A frail and bloody pomp which time has swept
In fragments towards oblivion. Massacre,
For this I prayed, would on thy sleep have crept,
Treason and Slavery, Rapine, Fear, and Lust,
And stifled thee, their minister. I know

Too late, since thou and France are in the dust,

That virtue owns a more eternal foe

Than force or fraud: old Custom, legal Crime,

And bloody Faith the foulest birth of time.

SUPERSTITION.

Thou taintest all thou lookest upon! The stars,
Which on thy cradle beamed so brightly sweet,
Were gods to the distempered playfulness
Of thy untutored infancy; the trees,
The grass, the clouds, the mountains, and the sea,
All living things that walk, swim, creep, or fly,
Were gods: the sun had homage, and the moon
Her worshipper. Then thou becamest, a boy,
More daring in thy frenzies: every shape,
Monstrous or vast, or beautifully wild,

Which, from sensation's relics, fancy culls;

The spirits of the air, the shuddering ghost,

The genii of the elements, the powers

That give a shape to nature's varied works,

Had life and place in the corrupt belief

Of thy blind heart: yet still thy youthful hands

Were pure of human blood. Then manhood gave

Its strength and ardour to thy frenzied brain;

Thine eager gaze scanned the stupendous scene,

Whose wonders mocked the knowledge of thy pride:

Their everlasting and unchanging laws

Reproached thine ignorance. Awhile thou stoodest

Baffled and gloomy; then thou didst sum up

The elements of all that thou didst know;

The changing seasons, winter's leafless reign,

The budding of the heaven-breathing trees,

The eternal orbs that beautify the night,

The sun-rise, and the setting of the moon,

Earthquakes and wars, and poisons and disease,

And all their causes, to an abstract point

Converging, thou didst give it name, and form,

Intelligence, and unity, and power.

SONNET.

FROM THE ITALIAN OF DANTE.

Dante Alighieri to Guido Cavalcanti.

GUIDO, I would that Lappo, thou, and I,
Led by some strong enchantment, might ascend
A magic ship, whose charmed sails should fly
With winds at will where'er our thoughts might wend,
And that no change, nor any evil chance,
Should mar our joyous voyage; but it might be,
That even satiety should still enhance
Between our hearts their strict community:

And that the bounteous wizard then would place

Vanna and Bice and my gentle love,

Companions of our wandering, and would grace

With passionate talk wherever we might rove

Our time, and each were as content and free

As I believe that thou and I should be.

TRANSLATED FROM THE GREEK OF MOSCHUS.

Ταν ἁλα ταν γλαυκαν ὁταν ὠνεμος ατρεμα βαλλῃ, κ. τ. λ.

When winds that move not its calm surface sweep
The azure sea, I love the land no more;
The smiles of the serene and tranquil deep
Tempt my unquiet mind.—But when the roar
Of ocean's gray abyss resounds, and foam
Gathers upon the sea, and vast waves burst,
I turn from the drear aspect to the home
Of earth and its deep woods, where interspersed,
When winds blow loud, pines make sweet melody.
Whose house is some lone bark, whose toil the sea,

Whose prey the wandering fish, an evil lot

Has chosen.—But I my languid limbs will fling

Beneath the plane, where the brook's murmuring

Moves the calm spirit, but disturbs it not.

THE DÆMON OF THE WORLD.

A FRAGMENT.

Nec tantum prodere vati,
Quantum scire licet. Venit ætas omnis in unam
Congeriem, miserumque premunt tot sæcula pectus.
Lucan Phars. L. v. l. 176.

THE DÆMON OF THE WORLD.

A FRAGMENT.

How wonderful is Death,

Death and his brother Sleep!

One pale as yonder wan and horned moon,

With lips of lurid blue,

The other glowing like the vital morn,

When throned on ocean's wave

It breathes over the world:

Yet both so passing strange and wonderful!

Hath then the iron-sceptered Skeleton,
Whose reign is in the tainted sepulchres,
To the hell dogs that couch beneath his throne
Cast that fair prey? Must that divinest form,
Which love and admiration cannot view
Without a beating heart, whose azure veins
Steal like dark streams along a field of snow,
Whose outline is as fair as marble clothed
In light of some sublimest mind, decay?
  Nor putrefaction's breath
Leave aught of this pure spectacle
  But loathsomeness and ruin?—
  Spare aught but a dark theme,
On which the lightest heart might moralize?
Or is it but that downy-winged slumbers

Have charmed their nurse coy Silence near her lids
  To watch their own repose?
  Will they, when morning's beam
  Flows through those wells of light,
Seek far from noise and day some western cave,
Where woods and streams with soft and pausing winds
  A lulling murmur weave?—

  Ianthe doth not sleep
  The dreamless sleep of death:
Nor in her moonlight chamber silently
Doth Henry hear her regular pulses throb,
  Or mark her delicate cheek
With interchange of hues mock the broad moon,

Outwatching weary night,
Without assured reward.
Her dewy eyes are closed;
On their translucent lids, whose texture fine
Scarce hides the dark blue orbs that burn below
With unapparent fire,
The baby Sleep is pillowed :
Her golden tresses shade
The bosom's stainless pride,
Twining like tendrils of the parasite
Around a marble column.

Hark! whence that rushing sound?
'Tis like a wondrous strain that sweeps
Around a lonely ruin

When west winds sigh and evening waves respond
In whispers from the shore :
'Tis wilder than the unmeasured notes
Which from the unseen lyres of dells and groves
The genii of the breezes sweep.
Floating on waves of music and of light
The chariot of the Dæmon of the World
Descends in silent power :
Its shape reposed within : slight as some cloud
That catches but the palest tinge of day
When evening yields to night,
Bright as that fibrous woof when stars indue
Its transitory robe.
Four shapeless shadows bright and beautiful
Draw that strange car of glory, reins of light

Check their unearthly speed; they stop and fold
    Their wings of braided air:
The Dæmon leaning from the etherial car
    Gazed on the slumbering maid.
Human eye hath ne'er beheld
A shape so wild, so bright, so beautiful,
As that which o'er the maiden's charmed sleep
    Waving a starry wand,
    Hung like a mist of light.
Such sounds as breathed around like odorous winds
    Of wakening spring arose,
Filling the chamber and the moonlight sky.

Maiden, the world's supremest spirit
    Beneath the shadow of her wings

Folds all thy memory doth inherit
  From ruin of divinest things,
    Feelings that lure thee to betray,
    And light of thoughts that pass away.

For thou hast earned a mighty boon,
  The truths which wisest poets see
Dimly, thy mind may make its own,
  Rewarding its own majesty,
    Entranced in some diviner mood
    Of self-oblivious solitude.

Custom, and Faith, and Power thou spurnest;
  From hate and awe thy heart is free;
Ardent and pure as day thou burnest,
  For dark and cold mortality

A living light, to cheer it long,
　　The watch-fires of the world among.

Therefore from nature's inner shrine,
　　Where gods and fiends in worship bend,
Majestic spirit, be it thine
　　The flame to seize, the veil to rend,
　　　Where the vast snake Eternity
　　　In charmed sleep doth ever lie.

All that inspires thy voice of love,
　　Or speaks in thy unclosing eyes,
Or through thy frame doth burn or move,
　　Or think or feel, awake, arise !
　　　Spirit, leave for mine and me
　　　Earth's unsubstantial mimickry !

It ceased, and from the mute and moveless frame
   A radiant spirit arose,
All beautiful in naked purity.
Robed in its human hues it did ascend,
Disparting as it went the silver clouds
It moved towards the car, and took its seat
   Beside the Dæmon shape.

Obedient to the sweep of aery song,
   The mighty ministers
Unfurled their prismy wings.
  The magic car moved on ;
The night was fair, innumerable stars
   Studded heaven's dark blue vault ;
   The eastern wave grew pale
  With the first smile of morn.

The magic car moved on.

From the swift sweep of wings

The atmosphere in flaming sparkles flew;

And where the burning wheels

Eddied above the mountain's loftiest peak

Was traced a line of lightning.

Now far above a rock the utmost verge

Of the wide earth it flew,

The rival of the Andes, whose dark brow

Frowned o'er the silver sea.

Far, far below the chariot's stormy path,

Calm as a slumbering babe,

Tremendous ocean lay.

Its broad and silent mirror gave to view

The pale and waning stars,

The chariot's fiery track,

And the grey light of morn

Tinging those fleecy clouds

That cradled in their folds the infant dawn.

The chariot seemed to fly

Through the abyss of an immense concave,

Radiant with million constellations, tinged

With shades of infinite colour,

And semicircled with a belt

Flashing incessant meteors.

As they approached their goal,

The winged shadows seemed to gather speed.

The sea no longer was distinguished; earth

Appeared a vast and shadowy sphere, suspended

In the black concave of heaven
With the sun's cloudless orb,
Whose rays of rapid light
Parted around the chariot's swifter course,
And fell like ocean's feathery spray
Dashed from the boiling surge
Before a vessel's prow.

The magic car moved on.
Earth's distant orb appeared
The smallest light that twinkles in the heavens,
Whilst round the chariot's way
Innumerable systems widely rolled,
And countless spheres diffused
An ever varying glory.

It was a sight of wonder! Some were horned,
And, like the moon's argentine crescent hung
In the dark dome of heaven, some did shed
A clear mild beam like Hesperus, while the sea
Yet glows with fading sun-light; others dashed
Athwart the night with trains of bickering fire,
Like sphered worlds to death and ruin driven;
Some shone like stars, and as the chariot passed
  Bedimmed all other light.

  Spirit of Nature! here
In this interminable wilderness
Of worlds, at whose involved immensity
  Even soaring fancy staggers,
  Here is thy fitting temple.

Yet not the lightest leaf
That quivers to the passing breeze
Is less instinct with thee,—
Yet not the meanest worm,
That lurks in graves and fattens on the dead
Less shares thy eternal breath.
Spirit of Nature! thou
Imperishable as this glorious scene,
Here is thy fitting temple.

If solitude hath ever led thy steps
To the shore of the immeasurable sea,
And thou hast lingered there
Until the sun's broad orb
Seemed resting on the fiery line of ocean,

Thou must have marked the braided webs of gold
  That without motion hang
  Over the sinking sphere:
Thou must have marked the billowy mountain clouds,
Edged with intolerable radiancy,
  Towering like rocks of jet
  Above the burning deep:
  And yet there is a moment
  When the sun's highest point
Peers like a star o'er ocean's western edge,
When those far clouds of feathery purple gleam
Like fairy lands girt by some heavenly sea :
Then has thy rapt imagination soared
Where in the midst of all existing things
The temple of the mightiest Dæmon stands.

Yet not the golden islands
That gleam amid yon flood of purple light,
Nor the feathery curtains
That canopy the sun's resplendent couch,
Nor the burnished ocean waves
Paving that gorgeous dome,
So fair, so wonderful a sight
As the eternal temple could afford.
The elements of all that human thought
Can frame of lovely or sublime, did join
To rear the fabric of the fane, nor aught
Of earth may image forth its majesty.
Yet likest evening's vault that faëry hall,
As heaven low resting on the wave it spread
Its floors of flashing light,

Its vast and azure dome;
And on the verge of that obscure abyss
Where crystal battlements o'erhang the gulph
Of the dark world, ten thousand spheres diffuse
Their lustre through its adamantine gates.

The magic car no longer moved;
The Dæmon and the Spirit
Entered the eternal gates.
Those clouds of aery gold
That slept in glittering billows
Beneath the azure canopy,
With the etherial footsteps trembled not,
While slight and odorous mists

Floated to strains of thrilling melody

Through the vast columns and the pearly shrines.

The Dæmon and the Spirit

Approached the overhanging battlement.

Below lay stretched the boundless universe!

There, far as the remotest line

That limits swift imagination's flight,

Unending orbs mingled in mazy motion,

Immutably fulfilling

Eternal Nature's law.

Above, below, around,

The circling systems formed

A wilderness of harmony,

Each with undeviating aim
In eloquent silence through the depths of space
Pursued its wondrous way.—

Awhile the Spirit paused in ecstasy.
Yet soon she saw, as the vast spheres swept by,
Strange things within their belted orbs appear.
Like animated frenzies, dimly moved
Shadows, and skeletons, and fiendly shapes,
Thronging round human graves, and o'er the dead
Sculpturing records for each memory
In verse, such as malignant gods pronounce,
Blasting the hopes of men, when heaven and hell
Confounded burst in ruin o'er the world:
And they did build vast trophies, instruments

Of murder, human bones, barbaric gold,
Skins torn from living men, and towers of skulls
With sightless holes gazing on blinder heaven,
Mitres, and crowns, and brazen chariots stained
With blood, and scrolls of mystic wickedness,
The sanguine codes of venerable crime.
The likeness of a throned king came by,
When these had past, bearing upon his brow
A threefold crown ; his countenance was calm,
His eye severe and cold ; but his right hand
Was charged with bloody coin, and he did gnaw
By fits, with secret smiles, a human heart
Concealed beneath his robe ; and motley shapes,
A multitudinous throng, around him knelt,
With bosoms bare, and bowed heads, and false looks

Of true submission, as the sphere rolled by,

Brooking no eye to witness their foul shame,

Which human hearts must feel, while human tongues

Tremble to speak, they did rage horribly,

Breathing in self contempt fierce blasphemies

Against the Dæmon of the World, and high

Hurling their armed hands where the pure Spirit,

Serene and inaccessibly secure,

Stood on an isolated pinnacle,

The flood of ages combating below

The depth of the unbounded universe

   Above, and all around

Necessity's unchanging harmony.

THE END.

www.ingramcontent.com/pod-product-compliance
Lightning Source LLC
Chambersburg PA
CBHW022142160426
43197CB00009B/1400